WHEN MOMMY AND DADDY GO TO WORK

by **JOANNA COLE**
illustrated by **MAXIE CHAMBLISS**

HarperCollins*Publishers*

When Mommy and Daddy Go to Work
Text copyright © 2001 by Joanna Cole
Illustrations copyright © 2001 by Maxie Chambliss
Printed in Singapore. All rights reserved.
www.harperchildrens.com

Library of Congress Cataloging-in-Publication Data
Cole, Joanna.
    When Mommy and Daddy go to work / by Joanna Cole ; illustrated by Maxie Chambliss.
        p.   cm.
    Summary: Carly is sad when her parents leave her at day care to go to work, but when reminded
that they'll be back later, she soon begins having fun with her friends.
    ISBN 0-688-17044-7
    [1. Day care centers—Fiction.   2. Parent and child—Fiction.]   I. Chambliss, Maxie, ill.   II. Title.
PZ7.C67346 Wf   2001   00-057254
[E]—dc21   CIP
                                                                                             AC

Typography by Robbin Gourley
1 2 3 4 5 6 7 8 9 10

First Edition

Hi! My name is Carly.
Here are my mommy and daddy.
And this is my horse, Oatis.
We are a family.

In the morning,
we get washed and dressed.

We talk and sing.
Then, after breakfast,
it's time to go.

Mommy and Daddy take
Oatis and me to day care.
They kiss me and say good-bye.
At first, I'm sad.

I don't want them to go.
Miss Terri says, "Don't worry, Carly.
Mommy and Daddy will come back later."

Soon we're having fun.
I play dolls with Sarah.
Jesse and Rosie paint pictures.

Elliot's diaper needs changing.
It's a busy day!

When I'm at day care,
Mommy and Daddy are busy, too.
Daddy works at a school.
Mommy works selling cars.
When I play in the sand with Jesse,
what is Mommy doing? I know!

Mommy is showing a car
to some nice people.

When I swing with Mr. Ken,
what is Daddy doing? I know!

Daddy is helping big kids learn to read.

Soon it is lunchtime.
I wonder what Mommy's having.
A sandwich? Maybe Daddy has pizza.
I'll bet they wonder what *I'm* having.

It's spaghetti and applesauce!
That's my favorite.
I think Oatis likes it, too.

After lunch, it's nap time.
Before I go to sleep,
Mr. Ken shows me pictures
of Mommy and Daddy.
"They'll come back later, Carly,"
he says.

Carly

Jesse

Our Families

After our nap, we go for a walk.
We have fun.

After our walk, we make airplanes.
Mine is blue.
Then, guess what?
I hear people coming in the door!

We get my coat, my bag, and Oatis.
And don't forget my airplane!
Then we're ready to go.

Do you know what?
Miss Terri and Mr. Ken were right.
Mommy and Daddy *did* come back.
They always do.

Tips for Parents

So you've found child care you trust, and your baby or toddler is doing well. Now you can relax and have peace of mind, right? Right! But it's still wise to expect some upset surrounding the separation. Here are suggestions to make the transition easier for you and your child.

Say good-bye. Establish a routine when leaving. Show a cheerful attitude and reassure your child that you'll be back.

Expect some upset. It's natural for most babies and toddlers to object—sometimes dramatically—when they are separated from parents. But usually the crying stops soon after the parent is out of sight. If your child usually has a good day, don't take the crying too seriously.

Make it easier. It may help to let the child do something *active* during the leaving routine, such as going to the window to wave as you leave or putting something in his cubby for you to see upon return.

When you return. Sometimes a child begins to cry or act up when he sees a parent at the door. It's usually not a sign that day care is bad for your child or that he doesn't love you anymore. It's probably just the opposite: He feels so comfortable with you that he can let out his feelings.

Quality time with you is important. If you are away all day, try to minimize long absences in the evenings. Your child has a right to your loving attention every day.

What about *your* feelings? Most parents feel some degree of anxiety, guilt, or sadness at leaving a baby or toddler. It's fine to have the feelings, but move on from there. If everything seems to be going well for your child, give yourself a break—having relationships with others adds richness to your lives.

Be optimistic. Take reassurance from the record: Researchers have found that, all other things being equal, children who have had quality child care turn out fine!